The Adventures of Scuba Jack
Copyright 2021 by Beth Costanzo
All rights reserved

There are many creatures in our planet's oceans, yet some of them are known for their sheer size and scale. One of those sea creatures is the **beluga whale**. Weighing around 3500 pounds and growing as large as 18 feet long, beluga whales are some of the most interesting creatures on our planet today.

Along with their massive size, beluga whales are known for their high-pitched calls. These calls are high-frequency noises that beluga whales use to communicate with each other. Through things like whistles and clicks, they help each other gather food and navigate the ocean.

You can find beluga whales in some of the coldest waters. Specifically, they like to spend the summer months in deep waters near Alaska, Canada, Greenland, and Russia. Like some other sea creatures, beluga whales migrate every year. Beluga whales migrate away from these locations to find open sea during the winter months. These migrations can be as long as 3700 miles!

Beluga whales have very distinctive bodies. They are one of the few animals that has a completely white or white-grey color. It has a very special tail fin that has a recognizable curve. If you see one beluga whale (or a pod of them) swimming in the ocean, you'll probably notice those tails right away.

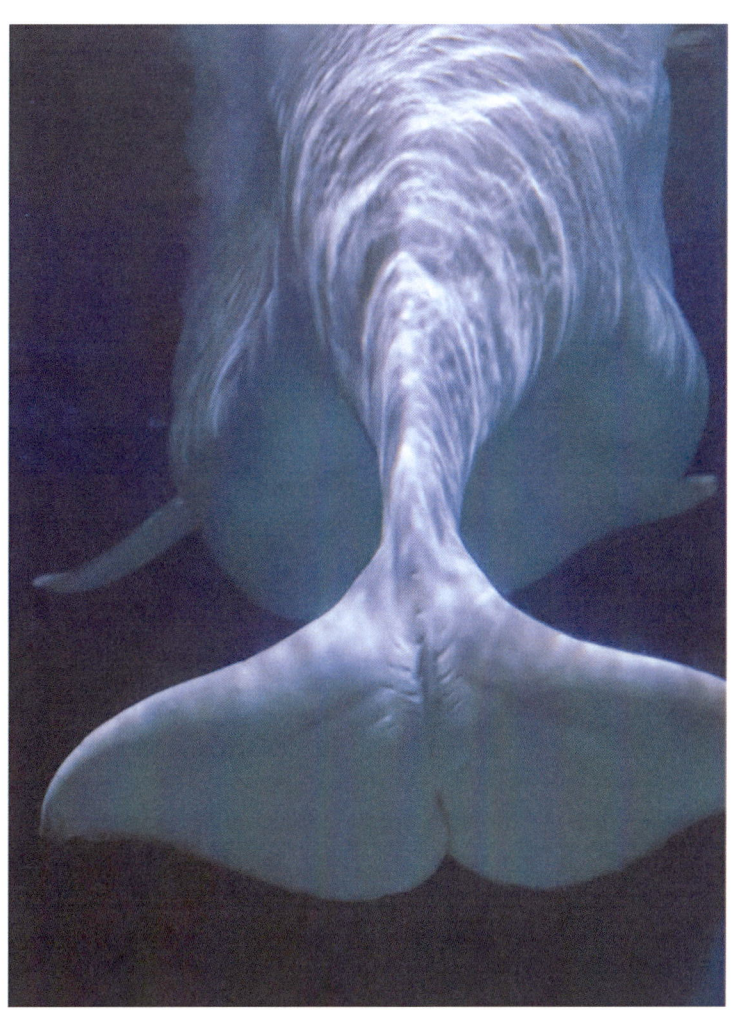

Ultimately, beluga whales are considered to be endangered. While you may see them in your local aquarium, there are fewer of them in the wild. As humans, it is our job to make sure that these fascinating creatures continue to swim in our world's oceans.

Fun Facts About Beluga Whale

- Beluga actually means "the white one" in Russian.

- The bump on the beluga's head is called a melon.

- Belugas can make up to 11 different sounds, such as chirps, whistles, cackles, and squawks.

- Beluga whales have a highly developed sense of hearing.

- Instead of using their teeth to chew their food, belugas use them to hold their prey.

- Belugas are curious and will swim around and under boats.

Beluga Whales Quiz

QUIZ

Write the correct answer in the box

How do Beluga whales communicate?

1- Turning around

2- High-frequency noises

3- Jumping

QUIZ

Write the correct answer in the box

How much do Beluga Whales weigh?

1- Around 2500 pounds

2- Around 5000 pounds

3- Around 3500 pounds

QUIZ

Write the correct answer in the box

Beluga Whales like ......

1- Cold Water

2- Warm Water

QUIZ

Write the correct answer in the box

Beluga Whales migrate every .....

1- Day

2- Month

3- Year

Beluga Whales Activities

Tracing Practice

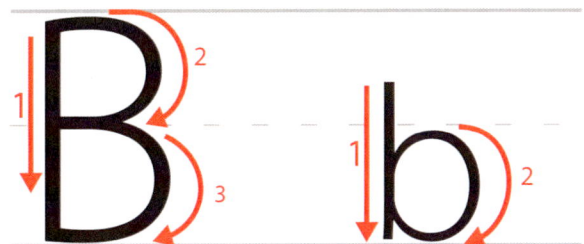

B E L U G A

W H A L E

Trace then rewrite the phrase below.

COUTING PRATICE

2 1 3 5

2 3 4 1

1 3 4 2

5 3 4 2

Count the beluga whales then circle the answer.

9 7 8	8 9 10
7 9 8	10 9 11

Maze

Help the Beluga to find its way

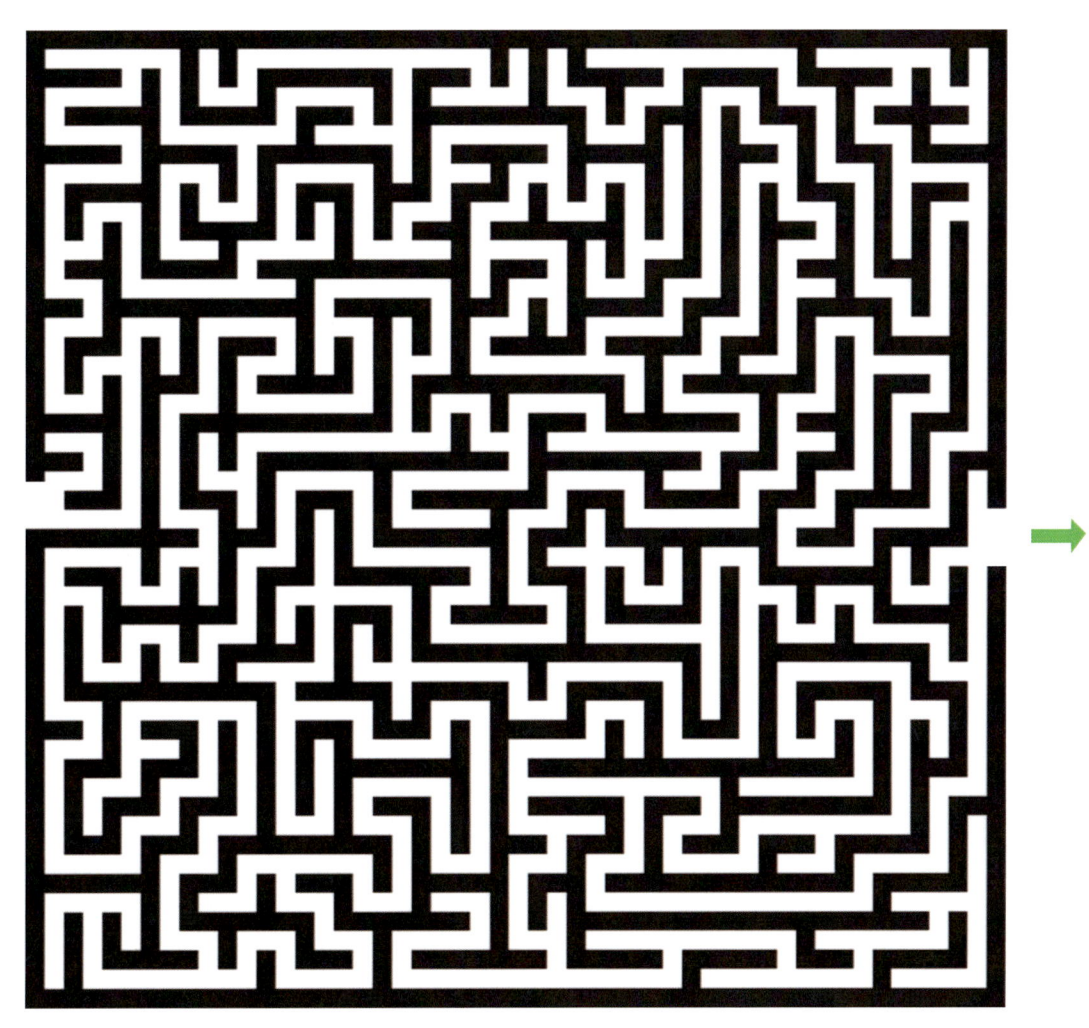

COLORING PAGE

Beluga Whales Craft

- Cut the Beluga's parts

- Glue the fins and tail to the body

- Draw the back face of the beluga

- Color your Beluga Whale!

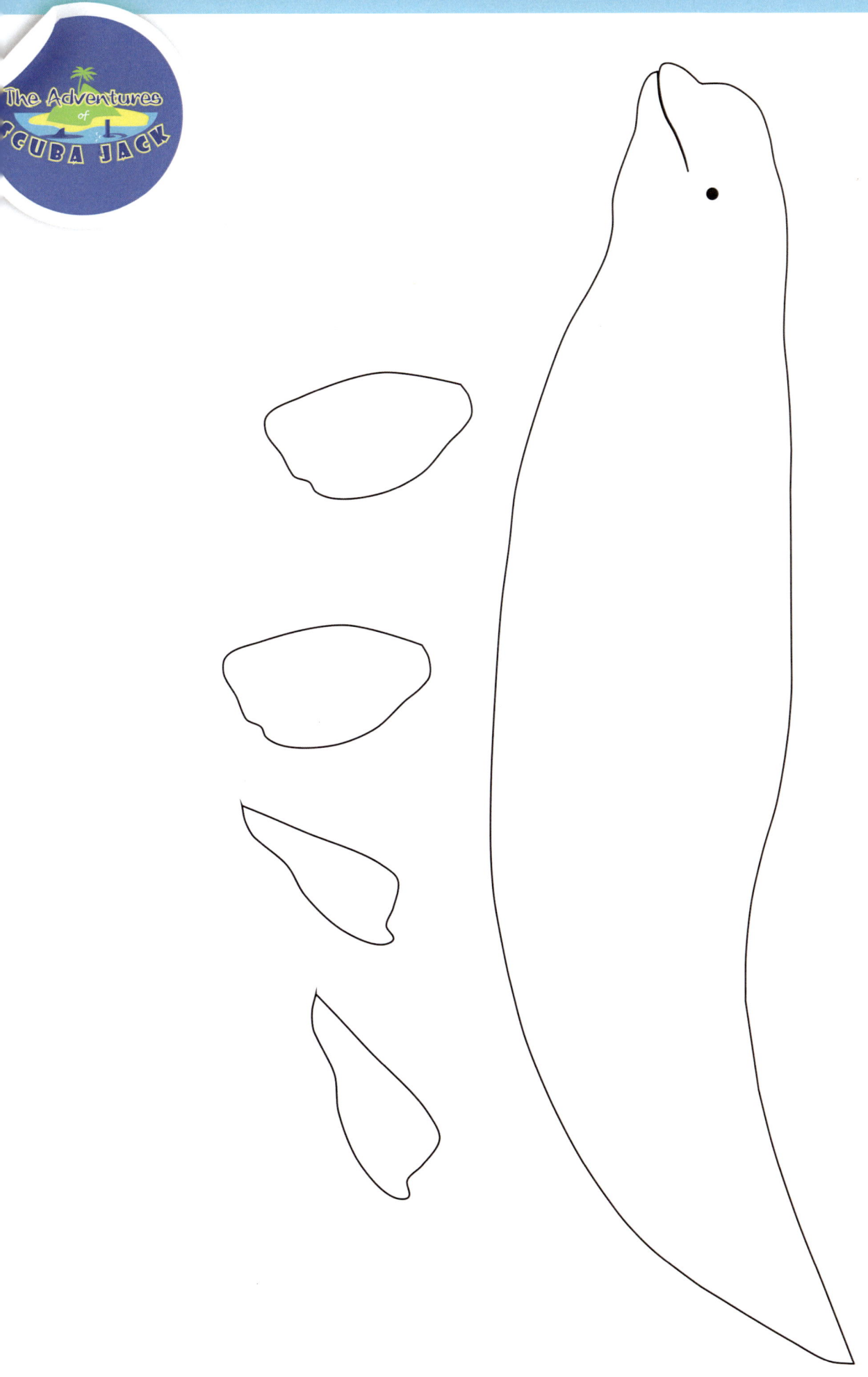

Visit us at:

www.adventuresofscubajack.com

www.ingramcontent.com/pod-product-compliance
Lightning Source LLC
Chambersburg PA
CBRC090838010526
44118CB00007B/246